Play With Big BOXES

Free
Fun
Unlimited

Play With Big BOXES

by

Liz & Dick Wilmes

Illustrations by

Carol Koeller

A BUILDING BLOCKS Publication

38W567 Brindlewood, Elgin, Illinois 60123

ART:

Cover and Text Illustrations:

Carol Koeller
Early Childhood Illustrator
Chicago, Illinois

Cover Design and Layout:

David VanDelinder
Studio 155
Elgin, Illinois

Text and Graphics Layout:

Karen Wollscheid
McHenry, Illinois

Special Thanks to:
Cheryl Airhart for inspiring us to include the WALK-ALONG VEHICLES. We hope that your children enjoy them as much as Cheryl's do.

PUBLISHED BY:

38W567 Brindlewood
Elgin, Illinois 60123

ISBN 0-943452-23-6

DEDICATED TO

ALL CHILDREN
WHO THINK
BIG BOXES ARE
WONDERFUL TO
PLAY WITH.

CONTENTS

Play Areas

Activity Booths

Easy Stages

Walk Alongs

Art

Learning Centers

PLAY AREAS

TEXTURE TENT

You'll Need

- Large, narrow box such as from big window panes or sheets of plexiglass
- 2 identical pieces of 10-15 different textured papers and fabrics (*sandpaper, furry fabric, corrugated cardboard, textured wallpaper, piece of carpeting, etc.*)

Make the TEXTURE TENT

1. Cut and fold the box into a tent shape.

2. Optional: Lay the "tent" in the art area. Let the children paint it with tempera paint and wide brushes.

3. Glue one texture from each pair to the inside of the tent. Glue the duplicate set to the outside of the tent.

Set-up the TEXTURE TENT

Set the TEXTURE TENT in a quiet place. Secure the edges to the floor with wide tape.

Add – Props and accessories as the children need them. You will soon discover that the children will use the tent for a variety of activities:

- Feeling the textures
- Reading
- Playing games
- More, more, more

Glue More "Things" To the Inside and Outside

- Duplicate sets of wide rubber bands, pencils, paper cups, pizza boards, bottle caps, paper clips, pom-poms, jar lids, egg cartons, etc.
- Different foot long pieces of string, ribbon, shoe laces, yarn, twine, rope, etc.

Last, But Not Least

Open up the TEXTURE TENT and hang it low on a wall so the children can see, feel, and talk about the objects one more time. Turn the board around and feel the other side.

BOOK NOOK

You'll Need

- Tall sturdy box such as from a refrigerator or large file cabinet
- Tempera paint
- Wide brushes
- Big pillows
- Fluffy throw rug
- Several stuffed animals

Make the BOOK NOOK

1. Cut off one long side of the appliance box.

2. Optional: Cut off the "roof" of the BOOK NOOK if the box is too shallow for the children to comfortably sit in.

3. Have the children put on their paint smocks and paint the box. Let dry.

Set Up the BOOK NOOK

After the box is thoroughly dry, set it in a quiet area, possibly near the book shelf.

Add – Several pillows, a cozy throw rug, and several teddy bears or other stuffed friends. Each day put 4-5 books/magazines in the BOOK NOOK which you think your children would enjoy.

Encourage the children to relax and:

- Look through a magazine.
- Do a puzzle.
- Read a favorite book.
- Tell a story to a teddy bear.

MINI BOOK NOOKS

(Use this idea for individual BOOK NOOKS.)

You'll Need

- Several rectangular or cylindrical boxes large enough for one or two children to comfortably sit in
- Wallpaper/patterned adhesive paper

Make the MINI BOOK NOOK

1. **Cylinder Boxes** – Cut openings in the cylinder boxes so that children can easily get in and out of them.

2. **Rectangular Boxes** – If necessary, cut down the rectangular boxes so that children can easily step in and out of them.

3. Cover the boxes with wallpaper/patterned adhesive paper.

Set Up the MINI BOOK NOOKS

Set the MINI-BOOK NOOKS around the room in areas where children want to be quiet and are likely to read and do individual activities – manipulative shelf, book shelf, language area, art etc.

Add – Soft blankets, small pillows, and stuffed animals.

VEGETABLE STAND

You'll Need

- Tall, sturdy box such as from a refrigerator or large file cabinet
- Chairs
- One color tempera paint
- Wide paint brushes

Make the VEGETABLE STAND

1. Have the children put on their paint smocks and paint all sides of the box. Let dry.
2. On a long strip of shelf/butcher paper write the name of the vegetable stand and glue it on the front of the stand.

Set Up the VEGETABLE STAND

Put the VEGETABLE STAND in an open area of your classroom.

Add – Vegetable stand props and accessories as the children need them. Here are a few suggestions:

Props

Plastic fruit and vegetables
Vegetable boxes/ baskets
Cash register
Money
Small tablets
Pencils
Bags
Price list
Child-size brooms
Wagon and/or wheel barrow

Clothes
Aprons
Wallets
Straw hats
Baseball hats

ADD A PUMPKIN PATCH TO THE VEGETABLE STAND

You'll Need

- Real or artificial pumpkins
- Rocking chair
- Scarecrow
- Hay bales

Set Up the PUMPKIN PATCH

Put the PUMPKIN PATCH near the vegetable stand. Let the children pick their pumpkins and pay for them at the vegetable stand.

You could also:

- Set up a pumpkin carving activity.
- **Explore the Pumpkin** – Cut a pumpkin in half. Set it on a large tray. Set the tray on a table Have an unbreakable bowl, tweezers, and several magnifying glasses on the table. Encourage the children to use their senses to learn all they can about the insides and outsides of pumpkins.
- Bake pumpkin seeds for snack.

STARRY NIGHT

You'll Need

- Large box such as from a double mattress
- White and yellow construction paper
- String
- Pillows

Make the STARRY NIGHT

1. If necessary, cut the box so that it is about one foot deep. Put it in an open area of your classroom.

2. Make all sizes of construction paper stars. Punch a hole in the top of each one and hang them from your ceiling so they float over the box.

3. Make other things that children will probably see in the night sky – moon, airplanes, etc. *(Make the moon in the shape it is when you do this activity. If it changes while the activity is going on, talk with the children about the moon. Change the shape hanging from your ceiling.)*

Set Up the STARRY NIGHT

Lay the box under the night sky. Put the pillows in it so it is comfortable to lie in. Encourage the children to lie in the box and stare up at the sky. What do they see? Where are the large stars? Small ones? Very tiny ones?

Add – Sky props and accessories as the children need them. For example you could add toilet paper binoculars, paper towel roll telescopes, and posters of the night sky.

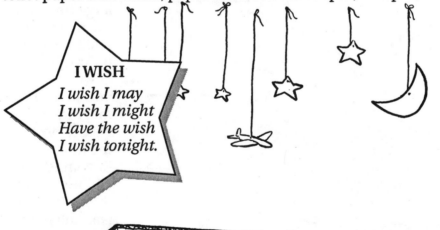

I WISH

I wish I may
I wish I might
Have the wish
I wish tonight.

Play I WISH – One day have a covered can and slips of paper/pencil near the night sky. Teach the children the I WISH rhyme. When they are looking at the STARRY NIGHT, have them say the rhyme and then make a wish. If they would like you to write it down, write what they say on a slip of paper and put it in the covered can.

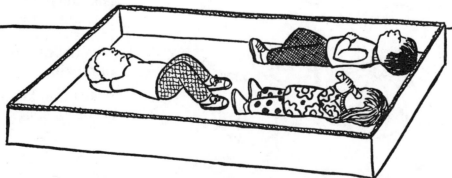

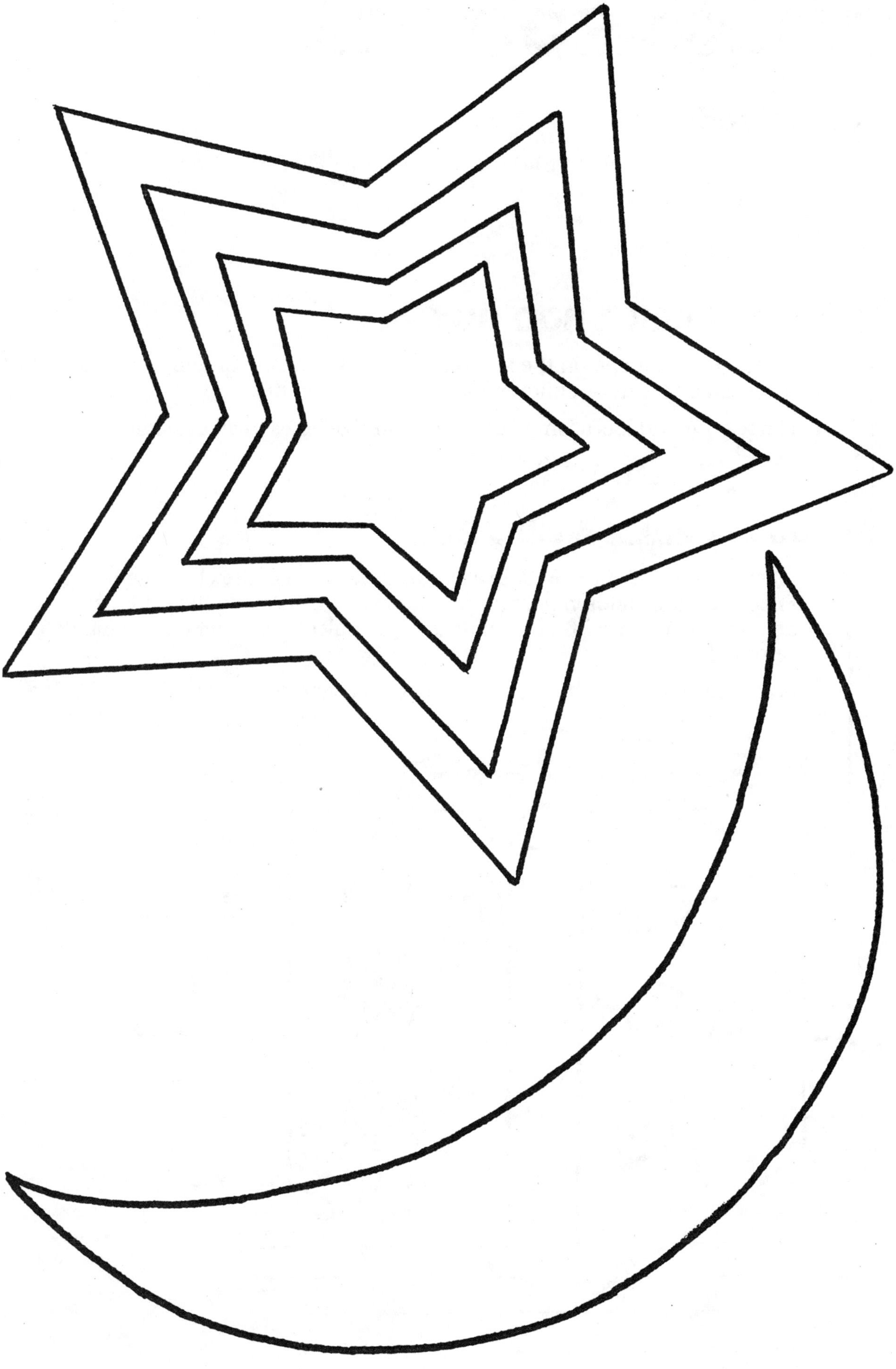

PLAY AREAS

PEEK-A-BOO BOX

You'll Need

- Sturdy appliance box, about the size of a washing machine carton
- Tempera paint
- Wide paint brushes

Make the PEEK-A-BOO BOX

1. Set the box on newspaper in the art area. Have several trays of tempera paint with a brush in each one. Let the children paint their box. Let dry.

2. Cut a large door and lots of small and medium size holes in all the sides and roof of the box.

Set-up the PEEK-A-BOO BOX

Place the PEEK-A-BOO BOX in a less travelled area of the classroom. Encourage the children to crawl inside and look out the different holes. What do they see? What are their friends doing? Look out another hole. What do they see now?

Add – Put some paper towel rolls in a bucket. Hang several pair of binoculars made with toilet paper rolls on the walls. Put a couple of low stools in the BOX so children can sit by one of the holes and relax as they watch what is going on in the classroom. Another time take out the stools and add several throw rugs or soft door mats.

Play Games With the Children

◈ Get a puppet, squat down next to one of the larger openings and talk with the children who are inside the box.

◈ Play WHAT'S ON THE FLOOR. Have the children lie in the box and look out the holes near the bottom of the box. What do they see?

◈ Play PEEK-A-BOO through the holes.

TELEPHONE BOOTH

You'll Need

- 2 or 4 identical large sturdy boxes such as from tall file cabinets
- Posterboard
- 2 or 4 lightweight wall telephones
- Large self adhesive Velcro®
- Wide sturdy tape

Make a Bank of TELEPHONE BOOTHS

(for each bank you'll need 2 boxes)

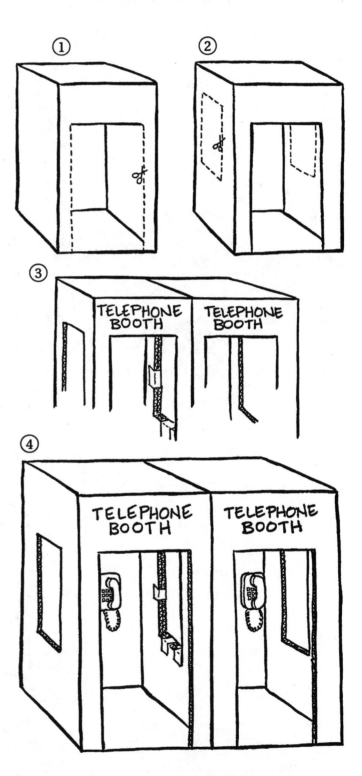

1. The 2 widest sides of the boxes will be the front and back sides of each telephone booth. Cut a wide door in the front side of each box.

2. Cut identical long narrow windows in the 2 narrow sides of each box.

3. Print "Telephone Booth" along the top front side of each booth. Put the 2 boxes side by side so the windows on the two boxes match up. Tape them together along the edges of the windows.

4. Put the "hook" side of 4-6 Velcro® dots on the backside of each telephone cradle. Decide where you want to hang the phone in each box. *(Easy height for children to reach.)* Put the "loop" side of the Velcro® dots on the box, so they match the "hooks" you just put on the telephone cradles. Stick the telephone to the box. *(Add more Velcro® dots if necessary.)*

5. Repeat for each bank of telephones you want in the room.

Set Up the **TELEPHONE BOOTH**

Set the TELEPHONE BOOTH against as wall. Use wide tape to secure the BOOTH to the wall and floor.

◈ Let the children stand in the phone booths and make as many calls as they would like.

◈ Other times a child/adult could stand in each booth and talk to each other through the windows.

Add –

◈ **911 Posters** – Write "911" in large bold letters on a piece of posterboard – one for each phone booth. Tack them on the walls, next to the phones. An adult/child stands in one booth, pretending to be the emergency operator, and a child in the other. Encourage the child to practice dialing 911 and then telling the operator what the emergency is. The operator can ask the child questions such as where the fire is – can try to calm the child by reassuring him that help is on the way, etc.

◈ **Simple Phone List** – Make a phone list with the children. Put all the names and numbers on it they would like. Draw a small picture next to each number so they know who they are calling. Duplicate the list for each phone. Hang one list at the children's eye level in each booth.

SCHOOL BUS

You'll Need

- Large box such as from a refrigerator
- Yellow and black tempera paint
- Wide brushes
- Chairs
- Sturdy paper plate
- Key on a key chain
- Long metal brad

Make the SCHOOL BUS

1. Lay the box on the art area floor. Cut one of the large sides off the box. This will be the roof of the bus.

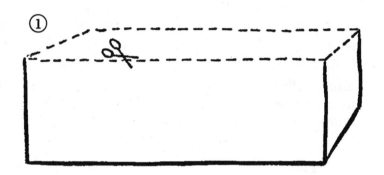

2. Have the children put on their smocks and paint the bus yellow. Let dry.

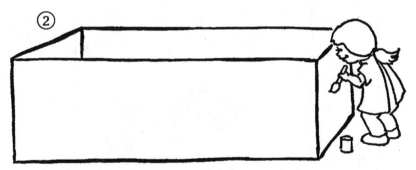

3. Using black paint, add headlights, a license plate, and any other "trim" you want.

   Cut:

   - A large window in the front of the bus for the driver.
   - A long door near the front.
   - Windows along the 2 sides.
   - A tiny slit near the steering wheel for the bus key.

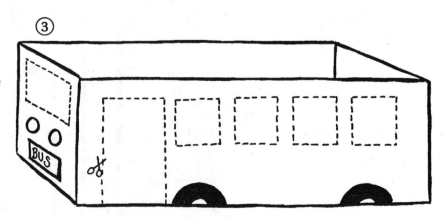

4. Paint "School Bus" along the sides of the bus.

5. Use a long metal brad to attach the paper plate steering wheel to the inside of the bus.

Set Up the SCHOOL BUS

Set the SCHOOL BUS in an open area of the classroom. Put chairs inside the bus. Fasten a large belt around each seat. Let the children use the SCHOOL BUS to go from home to school as often as they would like.

Add

Going Home – Backpacks, tote bags, and a bus driver hat. Ride the bus with the children and talk about all the things they did in school that day, what they are going to do when they get home, their favorite television programs, etc. You can also sing lots of their favorite songs – start with OLD McDONALD.

City Bus – Put several infant car seats on the bus. Have purses and hats, shopping bags, diaper bags, and dolls. Take trips around the town. Where are you going? What will you do there? Maybe you could sing WHEELS ON THE BUS to all the babies.

RAINY DAY PLAYHOUSE

You'll Need

- Appliance box about the size of a large stove
- Different colors of tempera paint
- Easel brushes
- Fabric
- Large self-adhesive dots
- Pillow

Make a RAINY DAY PLAYHOUSE

1. Paint the Playhouse – Lay newspaper on the floor in the art area. Set the box on newspaper. Pour shallow amounts of tempera paint into small containers. Have a brush for each container. Have the children dip their brushes in the paint and press them near the top of the box. The paint will squeeze out of the brushes and drip down the sides of the box. Some children may also want to dot the HOUSE with all colors of raindrops. Let dry.

2. Cut a large door in the front side of the box and several large windows, at the children's eye level, on the sides.

3. Make simple curtains by cutting fabric the size of the windows and taping it to them.

4. Make the inside comfortable by adding a few pillows.

Set Up the RAINY DAY PLAYHOUSE

Set the PLAYHOUSE against a wall so that it is available, but out of the way of regular movement.

Add – Playhouse props and accessories as the children need them for the activities they want to do, such as:

🔷 Just sitting on pillows/floor and talking to each other.

🔷 Playing with their dolls.

🔷 Playing games on trays or the floor.

🔷 Having pretend snacks and meals.

🔷 Going to sleep.

REFRESHMENT STAND

You'll Need

- Large tall box such as one from a refrigerator or wide tall file cabinet
- Tempera paint
- Wide brushes
- Butcher/plain shelf paper
- Jumbo marker

Make the REFRESHMENT STAND

1. Lay the box horizontally on the floor. Wrap a long piece of butcher/shelf horizontally around it. Tape it to the box.

2. In large letters, print "Refreshment Stand" across the front of the box. On one end print "Snacks" and on the other end print "Drinks."

3. Put the box in the art area and let the children paint it. Let dry.

Set Up the REFRESHMENT STAND

Put the REFRESHMENT STAND in an open area of the room or outside.

Add – Food stand props and accessories as the children need them. Here are several to begin with.

Props
Pitchers
Small paper cups
Several serving bowls for the snacks
    Fruit
    Sandwiches
    Breads
Menu *(optional)*
Tongs
Plates
Waste basket
Cash register
Money

Clothes
Aprons
Hats
Disposable gloves

🔹 **Prepare Food** – Let the children make and serve snacks and drinks.

🔹 **Serving Snacks** – Put a small table and several chairs near the REFRESHMENT STAND. Encourage the children to order drinks and snacks, and then sit around the table and "eat" them. *(The children may need pads and pencils to take orders and small trays to carry food.)*

🔹 **Take a Walk** – Have several small wagons and dolls. Let the children take their dolls for walks. They could stop at the REFRESHMENT STAND for a rest and snack.

🔹 **Snack Time** – On days that you are having a simple snack, add a tablecloth and set the food on the REFRESHMENT STAND. Let the children serve themselves from there. *(HINT – Have the drinks on the tables rather than at the REFRESHMENT STAND.)*

GAS PUMP

You'll Need

- Tall sturdy box such as from a 3-4 drawer file cabinet
- Butcher paper
- 2 pieces of old hose with nozzles

Make the GAS PUMP

1. Measure the front of the box. Cut a piece of butcher paper to fit on the front side.

2. Write the gas information on the paper. *(See illustration.)*

3. Glue/tape the paper to the front side of the box.

4. Cut a small round opening towards the bottom of one side of the box. Stick the hose in the opening. Securely tape the hose to the box.

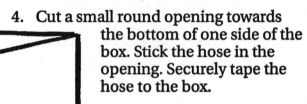

BUILDING BLOCKS GAS

GAS

REG-ULAR	SUPER	SUPER DUPER
1.00	1.10	1.20

PUSH BUTTON ☒ ☒

THANK YOU

Set Up the GAS PUMP

Set the GAS PUMP against a wall in the large motor or block area. Use wide tape to secure the PUMP to the wall and floor. Let the children use the riding toys normally kept in the classroom. As the children are riding, remind them to stop for gas.

Add – Gas props and accessories as the children need them.

🔹 **Riding Through Town**

- Make roads throughout the classroom with colored tape.

- Section off a small area of the room for a parking lot. Put the vehicles in the lot. When children are finished riding, they need to park their vehicles.

- Have several stop signs along the way.

- Make several driver's licenses and put them in wallets. When a child wants to take a drive, he needs to come to you and get a license. If a license and vehicle are available, he can ride; if all the vehicles/licenses are out, he'll need to wait.

- You could "police the drivers." Make "reckless driving tickets." If a driver is driving unsafely, you will talk to her and then give her a ticket. If any driver gets 2 tickets in a day, her license is suspended until the next day.

🔹 **Gas Station** – Add shirts, hats, a cash register, money, oil funnels, cleaned-out oil cans, rags, window scrapers, etc.

🔹 **Race Track** – Using colored tape, make a track in an open area of the room. Have a starting line, stop sign, and checkered flag.

🔹 **Outside Pump** – Have the children help you carry the GAS PUMP outside. Set it up near the outside riding toys. You might also want to have a CAR WASH near the pump. Make it simple with sponges and buckets of water. Great on warm days!

CAMPING TENT

You'll Need

- Large, narrow box such as from big window panes or sheets of plexiglass
- Tempera paint
- Wide brushes

Make the CAMPING TENT

1. Cut the excess cardboard off the box, so that two large attached sides are left.
2. Lay the giant sheet of cardboard flat on the floor. Have the children put on smocks and paint their *"tent."*
3. After the paint is thoroughly dry, fold the box into a tent shape.

Set-up the CAMPING TENT

Set the CAMPING TENT in a quiet place. Secure the bottom edges to the floor with wide tape.

Add – Camping props and accessories as the children need them.

Props

"Toy" grill
Pots and pans
Large spoons
Sleeping bags/
blankets
Flashlights
Coffee pot
Picnic
supplies
Tin cups
Backpacks
Paper towel
rolls for "logs"

**Camping
Clothes**
Bandanas
Hiking boots
Sunglasses
Sun visors

Soon Children Will Use the TENT for a Variety of Activities

- Sleeping in the sleeping bags.
- Cooking, telling stories, and singing around campfires.
- Taking hikes.
- Reading magazines in the tent.

SAIL BOAT

You'll Need

- Large rectangular appliance box
- 2 dowel rods
- Large piece of paper/fabric
- Tempera paint

Make the SAILBOAT

1. Lay the box on one of the long sides. Cut it down so that it is the right height for the children to climb in and out of, as well as sit in comfortably. Let the children paint it. Let dry.

2. Cut the posterboard/fabric into a large rectangular sail. Let the children paint it. Let dry.

3. Attach the ends of the sail to two dowel rods, and tape them securely to the edges of the "boat."

Set-Up the Sailboat

Lay a large bed sheet in an open area of your room. Set the sailboat in the middle of the "water."

Add – Boat props and accessories such as paper towel telescopes, oars, empty food boxes, sailor caps, etc.

Go Fishing – Cut large construction paper fish and slip a metal paper clip on each one. Put the fish in the water all around the sailboat. Make fishing poles with magnets at the end of the strings. Have several fishing buckets. Let the children kneel/stand in the sailboat and fish. When they catch something, encourage the children to put the fish in the buckets or toss them back into the water.

ACTIVITY BOOTHS

PEEK-A-BOO FRIENDS

You'll Need

- Tall appliance box such as from a refrigerator
- 4"x 6" photograph of each child
- Construction paper
- Heavy fabric such as denim or corduroy
- Watered-down white glue or spray glue
- Full strength white glue
- Jumbo black marker
- Wide tape

Make the Activity Booth

1. Take a close-up photograph of each child. Develop them in a 4"x 6" format. Glue each photo near the bottom of a piece of construction paper. Write the child's name above his photo.

2. Cut as many 9"x 13" pieces of fabric as you have children.

3. Lay the box on the floor. Carefully cut it in half lengthwise. Keep one-half on the floor. *(Save the second half for another Activity Booth.)*

4. Kneel in the box, and in large letters print *"Peek-A-Boo Friends"* near the top of the box.

5. At the children's eye level, glue the framed photographs on all sides of the box.

6. Drizzle white glue along the top of a piece of fabric. Carefully lay it over the top edge of the first photo. Gently rub the glue to adhere the fabric to the box and top edge of the construction paper. Repeat for each photo. When you are finished, all the pieces of construction paper will be hidden.

Set Up the Activity Booth

Put the PEEK-A-BOO FRIENDS Activity Booth against the wall. Securely tape it to the floor and wall.

Play PEEK-A-BOO FRIENDS

(Great game for individual children or pairs/small groups.)

- **Getting To Know You** – Have a child/ren stand in the box, lift the pieces of fabric and look at the photographs of friends.

- **Guess the Friend** – Have a child/ren stand in the box and see if she can guess who is hiding behind each piece of fabric before she peeks. After she guesses, have her lift the fabric and see who it is. Continue with the other photos.

FULL OF APPLES

(Thank you Dawn Zavodsky, Schaumburg, Illinois)

You'll Need

- Square type appliance box such as from an oven
- Green, brown, and red pieces of poster board
- Package of at least 12 self-adhesive hooks
- Small basket with handle
- Green craft grass
- 2 carpet squares

Make the Activity Booth

1. Lay the box on the floor. Carefully cut it in half lengthwise so that the part you are going to use has about a 1 to 2 foot depth. *(Discard the other section.)*

2. Kneel in the box, and in large letters print *"Full of Apples"* near the top of the box.

3. Make the Apple Tree
   - Cut a large black poster board trunk. Glue it to the middle of the inside wall at the bottom of the wide side.
   - Cut a large green poster board tree. Glue it on the tree trunk.
   - Put as many self-adhesive hooks on the apple tree as possible. *(Leave room in-between for the apples.)*
   - Glue green craft grass around the bottom of the tree.

4. Make the Apples
   - Using the pattern, make as many red poster board apples as you have adhesive hooks.
   - Punch a hole in the top of each apple.
   - Put the apples in the basket.

Set Up the Activity Booth

Put the FULL OF APPLES Activity Booth against the wall. Securely tape it to the floor and wall. Lay 1 or 2 carpet squares in the box.

Play FULL OF APPLES

Let the child/ren kneel or stand on the carpet square, take the apples out of the basket, and hang them on the tree.

Extend the FULL OF APPLES Tree

- Enjoy the children's favorite apple finger plays.
- Make green and yellow apples to hang another time.
- Count the apples.
- Have an apple taste test.

> **BOX OF APPLES**
>
> *Box of apples, box of apples.*
> *Who has it now?*
> *Let's look around the group*
> *And see who takes a bow.*

Variation

More Fruit – Instead of hanging apples on the tree, hang other fruit that grows on trees – bananas, lemons, cherries, limes, oranges, grapefruit, etc.

RAKE THE LEAVES

You'll Need

- Tall appliance box such as from a tall file cabinet
- 4 used same color file folders
- Green, yellow, orange, brown, red used file folders/poster board
- Small bushel basket
- White glue

Make the Activity Booth

1. Lay the box on the floor and cut off one wide side.

2. Cut the 4 same color file folders into 4 different size bushel baskets. Glue the side edges of each bushel basket together. Glue the 4 bushel baskets on the large side of the box.

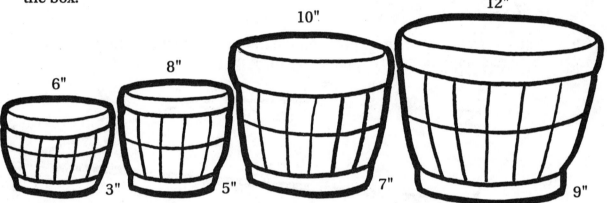

3. Using the colored file folders/poster board cut leaves in four different sizes *(giant, large, medium, small)*. Put the leaves in the bushel basket.

Set Up RAKE THE LEAVES

Put the RAKE THE LEAVES Activity Booth against the wall. Securely tape it to the floor and wall. Set the bushel basket full of leaves on the floor in the box.

Play RAKE THE LEAVES

- **By Size** – Let the children take the leaves out of the basket and sort them according to size – giant leaves in the giant bushel basket and so on.

- **By Color** – Glue red, green, yellow, and orange same-size file folder bushel baskets to an outside wall. Cut matching colored leaves. Put them in another small bushel basket and encourage a child to sort by color.

COLOR A PICTURE

You'll Need

- Tall narrow box such as from a refrigerator or tall file cabinet
- Wide tape
- White duplicating paper
- Spray glue
- 10 crayons
- Heavy yarn
- Jumbo black marker

Make the Activity Booth

1. Lay the box on the floor. Carefully cut off one wide side. Keep the box on the floor.

2. Kneel in the box, and in large letters print *"Color A Picture"* near the top of the widest side.

3. Very lightly spray glue on one piece of paper at a time. Tack it to one of the interior side walls so that it is within easy arms reach of your children. Keep adding paper *(space between each one)* until you've filled up the 3 inner walls.

4. Cut 10 pieces of yarn into 4 foot lengths. Tie each piece to a different color crayon. Tape the untied ends of the yarn to different areas in the box

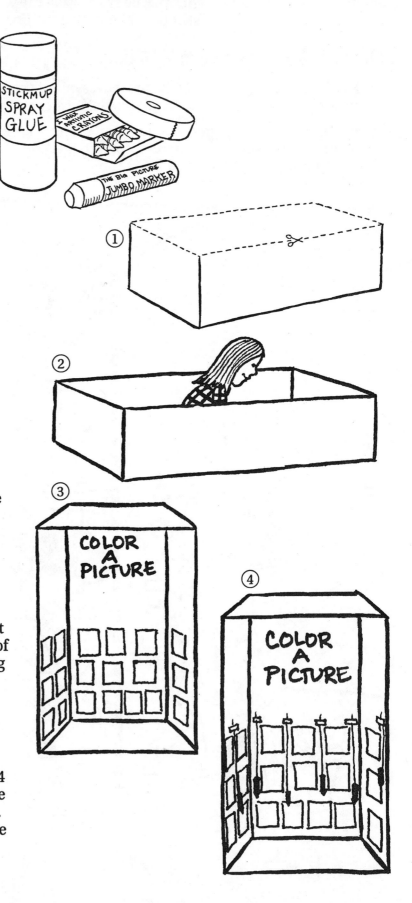

44

Set Up the Activity Booth

Keep the COLOR THE PICTURES Activity Booth against the wall. Securely tape it to the floor and wall.

COLOR A PICTURE in the Activity Booth

Let a child stand in the box, pick the paper he wants to color on, and then create any design, picture, or scribble he wants.

After all the paper has been colored, tack more paper to the 2 outside walls. Move the crayons from the inside to the outside, and let the children continue to color.

COL A PIC

TOSS THE BALLS

You'll Need

- Tall appliance box such as from a refrigerator
- Baseball wallpaper *(optional)*
- One or two drawer file cabinet box
- Lots of colored pompoms or beanbags
- Bucket for the pompoms/beanbags
- Jumbo black marker
- Wide tape
- White glue

Make the Activity Booth

1. Cut off one wide side of the box. *(Optional: Wallpaper the inside of the Activity Booth with baseball wallpaper.)*

2. Lay the box on the floor. Kneel in it, and in large letters print *"Toss the Balls"* near the top of the box. Using the black marker, draw 5-8 large baseball mitts under the title. With a pencil, draw a large circle in the middle of each mitt. Cut out the circles so there are openings in all the mitts.

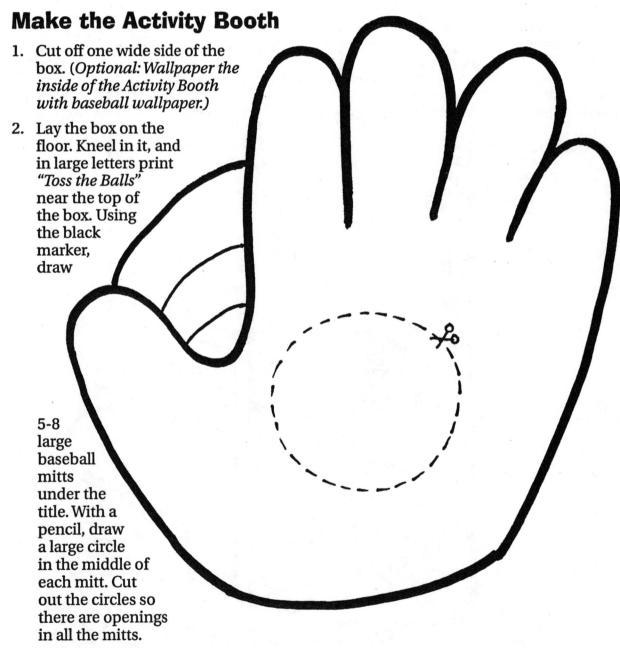

3. Cut the top off the small file cabinet box. Glue/tape it to the backside of the large box. *(This box will "catch" the tossed balls.)*

Set Up the Activity Booth

Put the TOSS THE BALLS Activity Booth against the wall. Securely tape it to the floor and wall. Put the buckets of pompoms/beanbags in the box.

Play TOSS THE BALLS

Let a child or several children pick pompoms/beanbags out of the bucket and toss them into the mitts. Keep tossing until all the balls have been "caught." Have the children take the bucket to the back of the box, retrieve the balls from the small box, and put them back in the bucket. Now they are ready to play TOSS THE BALLS again.

SHARE STORIES

You'll Need

- Square type appliance box such as from an oven
- 4-5 large sturdy shoe boxes
- Long narrow box such as from flowers
- Variety of small plastic/wooden people, trees, furniture, vehicles, animals, etc.
- Several carpet squares
- White glue
- Jumbo black marker

Make the Activity Booth

1. Cut off one wide side of the box. *(Save it for other activities.)*

2. Lay the box on the floor. Kneel in it and in large letters print "Share Stories" near the top of the box.

3. Kneel on the outside of the box. Glue 2 shoe boxes next to each other on the inside wide wall, about 2 feet up from the bottom. *(These are the stages.)*

4. About a foot above the shoe boxes glue the long box to the Activity Booth. *(This is the shelf for the props.)*

5. Optional: Glue one shoe box to the 2 outside narrow sides of the activity booth. *(These are extra stages for the children to use.)*

Set Up the Activity Booth

Put the SHARE STORIES Activity Booth against a wall. Securely tape it to the floor and wall. Put one or two carpet squares on the floor of the box. If you put stages on the outside of the box, lay a carpet square on the floor by each one. Set a basket of dramatic play pieces next to each carpet.

Have Fun SHARING STORIES

Encourage the children to use the various pieces as they create stories and situations and then share them with each other.

HAMMER THE PEGS

You'll Need

- Tall wide box such as one in which large panes of plexiglass and plate glass are shipped
- Large pieces of thick styrofoam
- Several wooden mallets
- Lots of golf tees
- Several pairs of safety goggles
- Small shoe box
- Sturdy "S" hook

Make the Activity Booth

1. Cut off one wide side of the box.

2. Lay the box on the floor. In large letters print *"Hammer the Pegs"* near the top of the box.

3. Glue the styrofoam on the wide side of the box at the children's level.

4. Securely tape the shoe box at the children's level to the side of the Activity Booth. Put lots of golf tees and several wooden hammers in the box.

5. Securely stick the "S" hook into the cardboard next to the box of golf tees. Hang the safety goggles on the hook.

Set Up the Activity Booth

Put the HAMMER THE PEGS Activity Booth against the wall. Securely tape it to the floor and wall.

Let the Children HAMMER THE PEGS

Let a child put on the safety goggles, and then take a hammer and pound golf tees into the styrofoam for as long as she wishes.

Variations

● **Hammer the Dots –** Use a dark marker and make lots of bold dots on the styrofoam. Let the children pound the golf tees into the dots.

● **Hammer and Hang –** Have a container of large size washers, along with the golf tees and hammers in the game box. After the children have hammered several tees into the styrofoam, encourage them to hang as many washers as they can off each tee. *Count them. How many? Is there the same amount on each washer? Can you put more washers on any of the pegs?*

● **More Hammering –** Instead of using golf tees, put wooden pegs, short pencils *(dull points)*, coffee stirrers, toy clothespins, and/or large paper clips in the game box.

CONNECT THE DOTS

You'll Need

- Tall narrow box such as from a refrigerator or tall file cabinet
- Wide tape
- Colored adhesive dots
- 5-6 dark crayons
- Heavy yarn
- Jumbo black marker

Make the Activity Booth

1. Lay the box on the floor. Carefully cut it in half lengthwise. Keep one-half on the floor. *(Save the second half for another Activity Booth.)*

2. Kneel in the box, and in large letters print *"Connect the Dots"* near the top of the box.

   Stand the box upright against an unused section of a wall.

3. Put colored dots all over the three interior sides of the box.

4. Cut 5-6 pieces of yarn into 4 foot lengths. Tie each piece to a different color crayon. Tape the untied ends of the yarn to different areas in the box.

Set Up the Activity Booth

Keep the CONNECT THE DOTS Activity Booth against the wall. Securely tape it to the floor and wall.

Play CONNECT THE DOTS

Let the children stand in the box, and use the crayons to connect as many dots as each would like. When most of the dots are connected, simply add more dots and let the fun continue. *(Keep adding more dots – there are never enough!)*

Variation

More Connect the Dots – At the beginning of the game, hang several penlight flashlights instead of crayons. Let the children CONNECT THE DOTS with flashlights. After several days, take the flashlights down and hang the crayons.

MAGNET FUN

You'll Need

- Tall narrow box such as from refrigerator or tall file cabinet
- Magnet board such as a:
  - Magnetized chalkboard
  - Large metal oil pan *(automotive department)*
  - Metal counter protector *(household department)*
  - Magnetic write and wipe board/dry erase board
- Lots of magnetic pieces – both commercial and teacher made
- 1 or 2 small long sturdy box/es to hold the magnetic pieces
- Wide tape

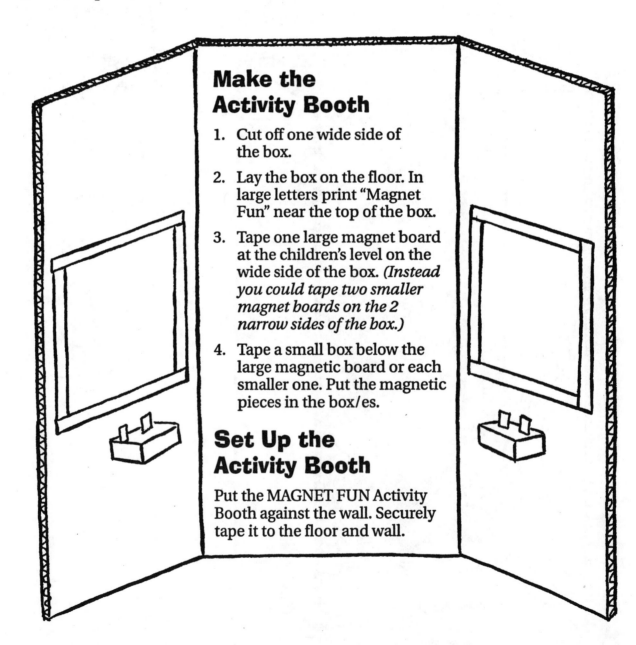

Make the Activity Booth

1. Cut off one wide side of the box.

2. Lay the box on the floor. In large letters print "Magnet Fun" near the top of the box.

3. Tape one large magnet board at the children's level on the wide side of the box. *(Instead you could tape two smaller magnet boards on the 2 narrow sides of the box.)*

4. Tape a small box below the large magnetic board or each smaller one. Put the magnetic pieces in the box/es.

Set Up the Activity Booth

Put the MAGNET FUN Activity Booth against the wall. Securely tape it to the floor and wall.

Play With the MAGNET BOARD/S

◆ **Set the Scene** – Have magnetic animal, children, nature, and building pieces in the box. Let the children create scenes and stories. Encourage them to tell each other about their creations.

◆ **What's the Number/Letter/ Shape?** Put magnetic letters, numbers, or shapes in the box. Let the children play games they create.

◆ **Magnetic Blocks** – Put magnet tape on colored inch blocks. Put the blocks in the box. Let the children build – make patterns – match colors – and more, more, more!

SLIP THE CHIPS

You'll Need

- Large "squarish" box such as from a stove
- Lots of poker and bingo chips
- Wide tape
- 2 sturdy shoe boxes to hold the chips
- Jumbo black marker
- Box cutter

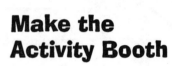

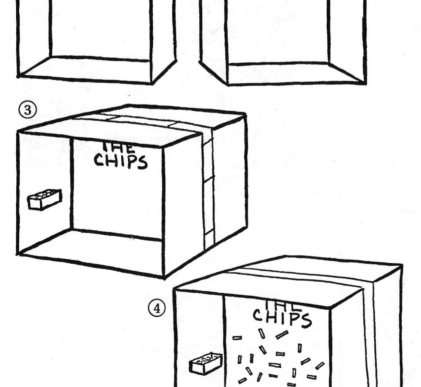

Make the Activity Booth

1. Cut the box in half length-wise. Print the title at the top of the largest side of each half.

2. Put the box halves back-to-back. Tape the 2 halves together.

3. Securely tape a shoe box at the children's level in each box. Put lots of chips in each box.

4. Carefully cut lots of horizontal and vertical 1 and 2 inch slits in both halves.

Set Up the Activity Booth

Place the box in an open area of the room. Securely tape it to the floor.

Play SLIP THE CHIPS

Have the children stand on each side of the box and slip different chips in and out of the slits. Let each child play for as long as each wishes.

Variations

🔷 **More Things** – Add other things to slip into the slits such as:

- Keys
- Colored plastic shapes *(Cut shapes from old plastic notebooks.)*
- Outdated credit cards *(Cut them in half.)*

🔷 **Slip the Clothespins** – After the children have slipped lots of flat things into the slits, use a large screwdriver and poke holes in both sides of the Activity Booth. Add colored clothespins and let the children slip the pins into the big holes.

🔷 **Slip the Pegs** – Use a small screwdriver and poke lots of small holes on both sides of the Activity Booth. Add colored wooden pegs or golf tees and let the children slip the pegs/tees.

DRESS "SPOTS"

You'll Need

- Tall appliance box such as from a refrigerator
- Tagboard
- All colors of poster board
- Used file folder
- Colored markers
- Jumbo black marker
- Wide tape
- Tempera paint
- Wide brushes
- White glue
- Box cutter/Exacto knife

Make the Activity Booth

1. Lay the box on the floor. Carefully cut it lengthwise so that the part you are going to use has about a 2 foot depth.

2. Put newspaper on the floor. Lay the box on it. Have the children put on smocks and paint the inside and outside of the box with lots of colors. Let dry. In large letters, with black paint, print *"Dress Spots"* near the top of the box.

3. Make "Spots"

   - On a piece of tagboard draw a large simple clown. Use colored markers to color his face and other features.

   - With a marker/s draw 26 circles on Spots' clown suit.

   - Turn the piece of tagboard over. Put a piece of tape *(same length as the diameter of each circle)* along the bottom of each circle you just drew.

   - Remember Safety: Turn the tagboard back over. Using an Exacto knife or box cutter, cut a slit just under each circle on the clown suit. *(The tape on the backside will strengthen each slit.)*

   - Draw and then cut out 26 different colored poster board circles the same size as the ones you drew on the suit.

4. Brush white glue along the 4 sides of the tagboard. Put it in the Activity Booth within the children's easy reach. Press down and let dry.

5. Make the pocket for the game pieces. Cut the file folder vertically in half so that it is about 4" deep. Glue the 2 side edges together. Glue the pocket on one of the narrow sides of the box. Put Spots' circles in the pocket.

Set Up the Activity Booth

Put the DRESS SPOTS Activity Booth against the wall. Securely tape it to the floor and wall.

DRESS "SPOTS"

Let the child/ren put the colored circles into the slits in Spots' costume. After he's all dressed:

🔷 Have the child/ren look for spots that are the same color

🔷 Point to and name the colors on Spots' costume

🔷 Rearrange the colors if they want

Variations

More Spots – Instead of making colored spots, make ones with:

- Numerals
- Shapes
- Letters
- Animals
- Etc.

MAKE A MATCH

You'll Need

- Large, wide appliance box, such as from a high dresser or large cabinet
- 2 pieces of poster board
- 2 identical sets of large stickers *(any type – mixed or a specific category)*
- 30 unlined 4"x 6" white index cards
- Lightweight fabric
- Watered-down white glue
- Jumbo black marker

Make the Activity Booth

1. Cut the Activity Booth

    - Lay the box on the floor. Carefully cut it lengthwise so the part you are going to use has a 1-2 foot depth. Keep that section on the floor. *(Save the other section for another Activity Booth.)*

    - Kneel in the box. In large letters print *"Make A Match"* near the top of the box.

    - Stand the box upright against an unused section of a wall.

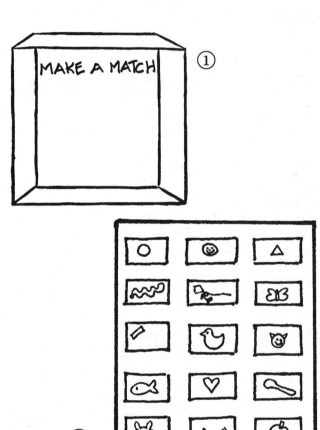

2. Make the Picture Boards

    - Evenly space 15 index cards on each piece of poster board. Put one set of stickers in the middle of each card on the first board. Put the other set of stickers, in a different order, in the middle of the cards on the second board. Glue all the cards down. Now you have two picture boards with identical stickers, but arranged in a different order.

    - Cut 30, 4"x 6" pieces of fabric. Drizzle a little glue along the top edge of the first piece of fabric. Lay it over the first index card. Press the glue down and let dry. Repeat for each index card so that all of them are covered and the stickers are hidden.

Set Up the Activity Booth

Put the MAKE A MATCH Activity Booth against the wall. Securely tape it to the floor and wall.

Play MAKE A MATCH

🎲 **Make A Match By Yourself** – A child opens a window on one board, looks at the picture, and then tries to remember where that identical picture is on the second board. She opens the windows until she MAKES A MATCH.

🎲 **Make A Match With A Friend** – The child lifts a window on her board. Her friend tries to remember where that picture is on his board. He lifts the window. When they make a match they can give each other a "hi-5." Switch. The second player lifts a window and the first child tries to remember where her matching picture is. Continue.

Variation

Name That Picture – Let a child open all the windows and name the pictures.

EASY STAGES

ON THE FARM

Make a Simple FARM STAGE

🧊 Large, shallow cardboard box such as a 15"x 30" under-the-bed storage box

🧊 Blue and green tempera paint

🧊 Wide black marker

Draw several roads for the farm vehicles to get from the home area to the barns and fields. Paint them black. Paint the land green. Once the paint has dried, paint several blue ponds on the landscape. (*Optional: Add other landscape features your children would like.*)

Farm Props

(Be flexible. As children play rotate props.)

Fences
House
Barns
People
Farm animals
Cars
Trucks
Tractors
Empty fruit/vegetable
   seed packets
Tiny bundles of hay

🧊 Put all the farm props in a smaller box. Store the prop box inside the big box.

Farm Costumes

Several neckerchiefs
Straw hats
Coveralls

🧊 Store the costumes in the big box.

Farm Activity

🧊 Build fences

🧊 Plant fields

🧊 Ride horses

🧊 Drive hay to the fields

🧊 Take animals to the fields

AT THE ZOO

Make a Simple ZOO STAGE

- Large, shallow cardboard box such as a 15"x 30" under-the-bed storage box
- Tempera paint
- Wide black marker
- White glue
- Sand

1. Draw sidewalks for people to walk around animal habitats and observe the zoo animals.

2. Paint the animal areas. For example paint the water animal area/s blue and the land animal area/s brown, yellow and/or green. Add ponds to each of the land animal areas.

3. Make a sandy area for the people to picnic and rest in. Brush a thin layer of white glue over the cardboard. Sprinkle sand on top of it.

Zoo Props

(Be flexible. As children play rotate props.)

Zoo animals
People
Fences
Stones and small rocks
Twigs
Miniature trees and bushes
Toys for animals to play with
Miniature tables and chairs
Small bundles of hay
Little bowls for animal's feed

- Put all the zoo props in a smaller box. Store the prop box in the big box.

Zoo Costumes

Zoo headbands

- Store the headbands in the big box.

Zoo Activity

- Feed the animals
- Talk with the animals in "animal talk"
- Walk around the zoo and look at all the animals
- Have a picnic
- Walk the animals around the habitats

AROUND TOWN

Make a Simple TOWN STAGE

- Large, shallow cardboard box such as a 15"x 30" under-the-bed storage box
- Tempera paint
- Wide marker

1. Draw the streets of the town. Paint them gray. Use a dotted yellow line to divide each road into two lanes.

2. Paint the town areas. For example, paint the park area brown, commercial areas gray, and residential areas green. You could have a blue river running through the town.

Town Props

(Be flexible. As children play rotate props.)

People
Community helpers
Pets
Variety of buildings
  (houses, stores)
Vehicles *(cars, trucks, emergency vehicles, railroads, motor cycles)*
Trees and bushes
Bridges
Safety signs

- Put all the town props in a smaller box. Store the prop box in the big box.

Town Costumes

Community helper hats

- Store the community helper hats in the big box.

Town Activity

- Drive around town
- Put out fire across town
- Take pets for walks
- Go shopping
- Talk to neighbors

66

AT THE BEACH

Make a Simple BEACH STAGE

- Large, shallow cardboard box such as a 15"x 30" under-the-bed storage box
- Blue tempera paint
- Sand
- Pebbles
- Very shallow box to fit in half the big box

1. Divide the stage in two sections, one for the water area and one for the sandy area. Paint the water area blue.
2. Fill the smaller shallow box with sand, shells, and pebbles. Set it in the sandy area.

Beach Props

(Be flexible. As children rotate props.)

Water vehicles *(boats, sailboats, barges, canoes)*
People
Fish, ducks
Seaweed
Shells
Miniature pails
Miniature scoops, rakes, funnels, molds, sieves

- Put all the beach props in a smaller box. Store the prop box in the big box.

Beach Costumes

Bathing suits to slip on over clothes
Sunglasses
Lifeguard headband
Empty containers of sun block

- Store all the costumes in the big box.

Beach Activity

- Sail their boats
- Fill and dump pails of sand
- Take walks on the beach
- Talk about beach safety
- Sift the sand
- Add water to dry sand

Extension

Go Fishing – Make a miniature fishing game with short fishing rods. Let children put fish in the water and then GO FISHING.

IN DINOSAURLAND

Make a Simple DINOSAUR LAND STAGE

- Large, shallow cardboard box such as a 15"x 30" under-the-bed storage box
- Yellow, green, brown, and blue tempera paint

1. Divide the stage into three sections, sand, grass, and water.
2. Paint the sand area yellow. The grass area green. The water area blue.

Dinosaur Props

(Be flexible. As children rotate props.)

Dinosaurs
Snakes, lizards
Plastic flowers, vines, ferns, cactus
Tree branches
Rocks
Leaves
Shells

- Put all the dinosaurland props in a smaller box. Store the prop box in the big box.

Dinosaur Costumes

Dinosaur Watcher headbands

- Store the headbands in the big box.

Dinosaur Activity

- Let the dinosaurs talk to each other
- Help the dinosaurs eat
- Walk around with the dinosaurs
- Compare the sizes and characteristics of the dinosaurs

IN THE DOLL HOUSE

Make a Simple DOLL HOUSE STAGE

- ⬡ Large, sturdy cardboard box such as a 15"x 30"under-the-bed storage box
- ⬡ Wide marker
- ⬡ Rug remnants, linoleum, tile *(optional)*

1. Use the marker to divide the bottom of the storage box into the basic rooms of the house. Leave openings in all the rooms for the doors.
2. Optional: Glue pieces of carpeting, linoleum, or tile to the floors.

Doll House Props

(Be flexible. As children rotate props.)

Doll furniture
Miniature People
Doll babies
Buggies
Vehicles

- ⬡ Put the doll house props in a small box. Store the prop box in the big box.

Doll House Costumes

Mom and Dad hats

- ⬡ Store the hats in the big box.

Doll House Activity

- ⬡ Take naps
- ⬡ Take babies for walks in miniature doll buggies
- ⬡ Have picnics just outside the house
- ⬡ Give the babies baths

AROUND THE AIRPORT

Make a Simple AIRPORT STAGE

- Large shallow cardboard box such as a 15"x 30" under-the-bed storage box
- Gray, black, yellow, brown, and green tempera paint
- Wide marker

1. Paint two or three different runways gray.
2. Paint the parking lot area black. Paint yellow strips for the parking spaces.
3. Paint the grassy areas next to the runways green.
4. Paint the hanger and terminal areas brown.

Airport Props

(Be flexible. As children rotate props.)

Airplanes
Blocks to make hangers and other buildings
Passengers
Airport workers
Cars
Buses

- Put all the airport props in a smaller box. Store the prop box inside the big box.

Airport Costumes

Pilot hats
Pilot badges

- Store the costumes in the big box.

Airport Activity

- Take-off, fly, and land the airplanes
- Have people drive to the airport, park, and ride the bus to the terminal
- Help the passengers board the airplane
- Load luggage

AROUND THE POND

Make a Simple POND STAGE

- Large, shallow cardboard box such as a 15"x 30" under-the-bed storage box
- Blue, green, yellow, and brown tempera paint   • Sand   • White glue

1. Draw a large pond in the middle of the box. Paint it blue.
2. Make a sandy bank along a portion of the pond. Brush glue in the area and sprinkle sand on it. Paint a muddy bank around the rest of the pond brown.
3. Paint the landscape around the pond green and yellow.

Pond Props

(Be flexible. As children rotate props.)

Plastic/rubber insects
Spiders
Snakes
Frogs
Ducks
Birds
Worms
Small branches
Rocks
Fish
Canoes
Row boats
People

- Put all the pond props in a smaller box. Store the prop box inside the big box.

Pond Costumes

Fishing hats

- Store the fishing hats in the big box.

Pond Activity

- Take a walk around pond
- Hunt for worms
- Fish
- Row boats around pond

WALK
ALONG

VEHICLES

FIRE ENGINE

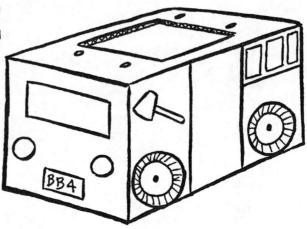

You'll Need

- 14"x 20" sturdy cardboard box
- Red, yellow, and black tempera paint
- Clothesline
- 4 aluminum foil pie pans
- 4 metal brads
- Optional: Pairs of high black boots and fire fighter helmets near the fire engine

To Make

1. Cut off the top of the box. *(This will be the bottom of the vehicle.)*

2. Turn the box over. Cut out a 10"x 12" section from the middle of the box for a child to slip his head and body through. *(Optional: Reinforce the four sides of the opening by gluing thin flat pieces of wood, such as paint stir sticks, to the underside of the edges.)*

3. Punch two holes on each side of the cut out section. Cut two, 4 foot pieces of clothesline for the straps. Loop the straps through the holes and tie a big knot at each end on the inside of the box. *(The box should hang around children's waists.)*

4. Paint the fire engine red. Paint the inside of the 4 aluminum pans black. After the red paint has dried, paint the lettering and detail yellow and black. Let dry.

5. Attach the pie pan wheels to the sides of the engine with metal brads.

POLICE CAR

You'll Need

- 14"x 20" sturdy cardboard box
- Black and yellow tempera paint
- Clothesline
- 4 aluminum foil pie pans
- 4 metal brads
- Optional: Have police officer badges and hats near the police cars

To Make

1. Cut off the top of the box. *(This will be the bottom of the vehicle.)*

2. Turn the box over. Cut out a 10"x 12" section from the middle of the box for a child to slip his head and body through. *(Optional: Reinforce the 4 sides of the opening by gluing thin flat pieces of wood, such as paint stir sticks, to the underside of the edges.)*

3. Punch two holes on each side of the cut out section. Cut two, 4 foot pieces of clothesline for the straps. Loop the straps through the holes and tie a big knot at each end on the inside of the box. *(The box should hang around children's waists.)*

4. Paint the police car black. After the black paint has dried, paint the lettering and detail on the police car yellow. Let dry.

5. Attach the pie pan wheels to the sides of the car with metal brads.

AMBULANCE

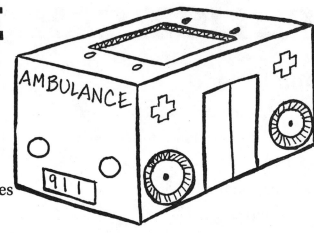

You'll Need

- 14" x 20" sturdy cardboard box
- White, red, and black tempera paint
- Clothesline
- Optional: White shirts near ambulances

To Make

1. Cut off the top of the box. *(This will be the bottom of the vehicle.)*

2. Turn the box over. Cut out a 10" x 12" section from the middle of the box for a child to slip his head and body through. *(Optional: Reinforce the 4 sides of the opening by gluing thin flat pieces of wood, such as paint stir sticks, to the underside of the edges.)*

3. Punch two holes on each side of the cut out section. Cut two, 4 foot pieces of clothesline for the straps. Loop the straps through the holes and tie a big knot at each end on the inside of the box. *(The box should hang around children's waists.)*

4. Paint the ambulance white. After the white paint has dried, paint the wheels black and the lettering and detail on the ambulance red and black.

TRAIN ENGINE

You'll Need

- 14"x 20" sturdy cardboard box
- Yellow, red, and black tempera paint
- Clothesline
- 8, 6" aluminum foil pie pans
- 8 metal brads
- Optional: Have engineer hats near the train engines

To Make

1. Cut off the top of the box. *(This will be the bottom of the vehicle.)*

2. Turn the box over. Cut out a 10"x 12" section from the middle of the box for a child to slip his head and body through. *(Optional: Reinforce the 4 sides of the opening by gluing thin flat pieces of wood, such as paint stir sticks, to the underside of the edges.)*

3. Punch two holes on each side of the cut out section. Cut two, 4 foot pieces of clothesline for the straps. Loop the straps through the holes and tie a big knot at each end on the inside of the box. *(The box should hang around children's waists.)*

4. Paint the train engine black. Paint the inside of the eight aluminum pans red. After the black paint on the engine has dried, paint the lettering and detail yellow.

5. Let the engine dry. Attach 4 pie pan wheels to each side of the engine with metal brads.

SCHOOL BUS

You'll Need

- 14"x 20" sturdy cardboard box
- Yellow, red, white, and black tempera paint
- Clothesline
- Optional: Have bus driver hats near the buses

To Make

1. Cut off the top of the box. *(This will be the bottom of the vehicle.)*

2. Turn the box over. Cut out a 10"x 12" section from the middle of the box for a child to slip his head and body through. *(Optional: Reinforce the 4 sides of the opening by gluing thin flat pieces of wood, such as paint stir sticks, to the underside of the edges.)*

3. Punch two holes on each side of the cut out section. Cut two, 4 foot pieces of clothesline for the straps. Loop the straps through the holes and tie a big knot at each end on the inside of the box. *(The box should hang around children's waists.)*

4. Paint the school bus yellow. After the yellow paint has dried, paint the wheels, lettering, and detail black and the windows white. Paint a large red stop sign on the side of the bus near the front.

MAIL TRUCK

You'll Need

- 14"x 20" sturdy cardboard box
- Red, white, blue, and black tempera paint
- Clothesline
- Small letter basket
- 2 "S" hooks
- Optional: Letter carrier hats near the mail trucks, and old envelopes and cards

To Make

1. Cut off the top of the box. *(This will be the bottom of the vehicle.)*

2. Turn the box over. Cut out a 10"x 12" section from the middle of the box for a child to slip his head and body through. *(Optional: Reinforce the 4 sides of the opening by gluing thin flat pieces of wood, such as paint stir sticks, to the underside of the edges.)*

3. Punch two holes on each side of the cut out section. Cut two, 4 foot pieces of clothesline for the straps. Loop the straps through the holes and tie a big knot at each end on the inside of the box. *(The box should hang around children's waists.)*

4. Paint the mail truck white, the wheels black, and the lettering and detail red and blue. Let dry.

5. Slip the bottoms of the 2 "S" hooks into the backside of the letter basket. Stick the tops of the hooks into the side of the truck. Put the mail in it.

AIRPLANE

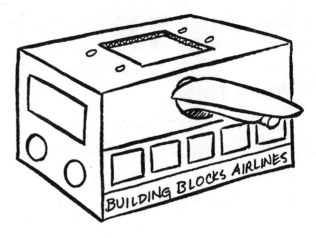

You'll Need

- 14"x 20" sturdy cardboard box
- Blue, yellow, red, and black tempera paint
- Clothesline
- Old child's dress shirt
- Large piece of cardboard
- Optional: Have pilot's hats and badges near the airplanes

To Make

1. Cut off the top of the box. *(This will be the bottom of the vehicle.)*

2. Turn the box over. Cut out an opening from the middle of the box large enough for a child to slip his head through. *(The box should rest on children's shoulders.)*

3. WINGS: Cut holes in the sides of the box for a child to slip her arms through. Cut the sleeves off the shirt. Slip one sleeve into each hole. Securely glue each one to the inside of the box. Cut 2 cardboard wing shapes. Glue one wing to each sleeve.

4. Paint the airplane blue. After the blue paint has dried, paint the lettering and detail yellow, red, and black.

DISPOSAL TRUCK

You'll Need

- 14"x 20" sturdy cardboard box
- Orange, black, and white tempera paint
- Clothesline
- Boot box/large shoe box
- 2 "S" hooks
- Optional: Waste hauler hats near the disposal trucks

To Make

1. Cut off the top of the box. *(This will be the bottom of the vehicle.)*

2. Turn the box over. Cut out a 10"x 12" section from the middle of the box for a child to slip his head and body through. *(Optional: Reinforce the 4 sides of the opening by gluing thin flat pieces of wood, such as paint stir sticks, to the underside of the edges.)*

3. Punch two holes on each side of the cut out section. Cut two, 4 foot pieces of clothesline for the straps. Loop the straps through the holes and tie a big knot at each end on the inside of the box. *(The box should hang around children's waists.)*

4. Paint the disposal truck orange. After the orange paint has dried, paint the headlights white and paint the wheels, lettering and detail black.

5. Slip the bottoms of the 2 "S" hooks into one long side of the shoe box. Stick the tops of the hooks into the back end of the disposal truck. Let the children collect the "garbage" as they drive around.

ART

BUDDY PAINTING

You'll Need

- One or more large, sturdy shallow box/es *(cut down if necessary)*
- Butcher paper cut in pieces to fit in bottom of box
- Several golf balls
- Tempera paint
- Margarine tubs
- Spoons/small scoops

Activity

Pour several different colors of tempera paint into margarine tubs. Put a golf ball and spoon/scoop in each one.

(Have 2-4 children enjoy this activity together.) Have them lay a piece of paper in the box, and then scoop one or more paint-filled golf balls into it. Each child hold onto a side of the box, and work together to roll the painted balls around. After a while, re-dip the balls in the paint, put them back in the box, and continue to BUDDY PAINT.

After each group of buddies is finished painting, write their names on the paper and help them hang it up to dry.

Another Time – Let the children use smaller boxes, duplicating paper, and ping pong balls, and do the activity by themselves rather than with buddies.

SIT AND COLOR

You'll Need

- Several boxes, each one large enough for a child to sit in
- Crayons

Activity

Put the crayons in several small boxes. Put one box in each large box. Set the boxes in a quiet area of the room.

Let a child sit or lie in a box. Have her use the crayons to color the inside and outside of the box. Leave the boxes out for several days until they are completely decorated.

Extension

By Myself - Use the boxes for individual activities, such as reading, writing, puzzles, thinking, resting, etc.

BOX PAINTING

You'll Need

- Large grocery box or appliance box
- Tempera paint
- Plastic pool
- Juice cans
- Wide brushes

Activity

Pour several different colors of tempera paint into 5-6 juice cans. Put the cans in a cardboard soda pop carrier.

Carry the supplies outside. Set the large box in the middle of the plastic pool, and the paint and brushes next to it. Have the children put on their smocks before they begin. *(To keep excess sand, dirt, etc. out of the pool, have the children remove their shoes and socks.)*

As the children want to take a break from active play, let them stand in the pool and paint the box.

ON-GOING BOX CONSTRUCTIONS

You'll Need

- Large sheet of heavy cardboard, such as from the side of an appliance box
- Variety of smaller boxes
- Glue and brushes

Activity

Lay the piece of cardboard on the floor in the art area. Have the boxes, glue, and brushes nearby. Let the children brush glue on one side of the boxes, and stick them to the base or to a box already glued on. Continue to glue and build for days. When finished, paint the structure.

Hint: Encourage the children to bring boxes from home each day, and glue them to the construction. *(It is so much fun to see the variety of boxes the children bring in, and how they incorporate them into their structure.)*

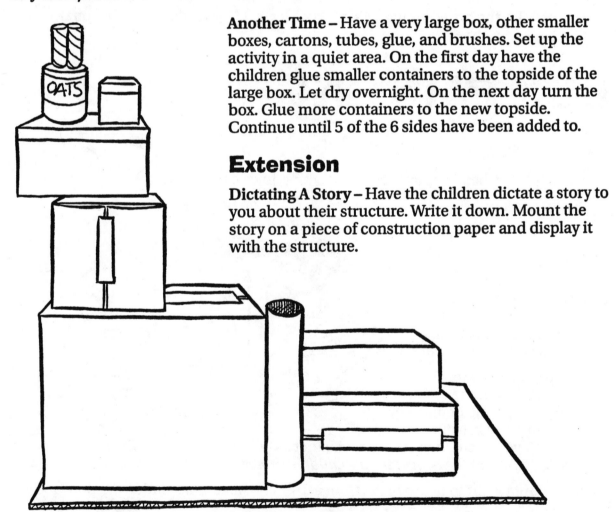

Another Time – Have a very large box, other smaller boxes, cartons, tubes, glue, and brushes. Set up the activity in a quiet area. On the first day have the children glue smaller containers to the topside of the large box. Let dry overnight. On the next day turn the box. Glue more containers to the new topside. Continue until 5 of the 6 sides have been added to.

Extension

Dictating A Story – Have the children dictate a story to you about their structure. Write it down. Mount the story on a piece of construction paper and display it with the structure.

GIANT MURAL

You'll Need

- Side of a large appliance box
- Tempera paint/brushes
- Car drink holders
- Juice concentrate boxes

Activity

Fill the juice concentrate boxes with different colors of paint. Add a brush to each. Put them in a soda container. Have a child carry the container outside. Clip the side of the appliance box to your playground fence. Hang the cup holders just below the cardboard. Put a container of paint in each cup holder. Let the children paint the mural.

DRIP PAINTING

You'll Need

- Children's socks
- Thick sponges
- Tempera paint
- Pie pans
- Large appliance box
- Newspaper

Make Giant Daubers

1. Cut the sponges into fairly large pieces to fit into the children's socks.
2. Put one sponge in the toe of each sock.
3. Tie the tops of the socks closed with rubber bands or pieces of yarn.

Activity

Cut one or two sides off your appliance box. Slightly water-down the paint. Pour each color into a pie pan. Put one or two daubers in each one. Lay newspaper on the floor so that it butts up to the wall. Set the side/s from the box on the newspaper, leaning up against the wall. *(Tape it to the wall if necessary.)*

Set the pans of paint on the newspaper. Have the children choose one or two daubers, wiggle them in the paint and then press them against the cardboard. Watch the paint drip. Re-dip the daubers or change colors and press again and again. *"Any colors mixing? What new colors are appearing?"*

88 After the DRIP PAINTING has dried, hang it on a wall in your block area.

PORTABLE EASELS

Make the EASELS

(for each one)

1. Get a sturdy medium size box. Cut the ends and two sides off.

2. Fold the box into a tent shape.

3. Clip two clothespins to each side of the easel.

4. Cut paper to fit the easel.

Activity

Tape an easel to each end of your art table. Put the paper in the center of the table. Put shallow bowls of paint in front of each side of each easel. Let the children clip their paper to the easel and paint. When finished, have them hang their paintings to dry.

EASY EASEL PAPER RACK

Make the RACK

1. Empty the box that the easel paper came in.

2. Carefully cut one of the very narrow side edges off the box.

3. Carefully cut a 5" piece off the top of one side large side.

4. Let the children paint the box.

Hang the RACK

Have a second person hold the RACK on a wall close to the easels. Use pieces of wide tape to attach the RACK to the wall. Place 15 or more sheets of easel paper in the box so they stick out.

Activity

When the children want to easel paint, they can easily get a sheet of paper out of the RACK and set up the activity by themselves.

Extension

Construction Paper Container – Get a large clothes detergent box. *(They are very sturdy.)* Cut the top off. *(Optional: Cover with patterned adhesive paper.)* Put a variety of colors of construction paper in the box. Set the box on the art table so it's immediately available for all the "artists."

ART BOX

Make the ART BOX

1. Check your local grocery store for a heavy-duty divided box, such as one that large glass bottles come in.

2. Cut the box so that it is about six inches high.

3. Glue an accordion folder to the side of the box.

Activity

Fill the accordion folder with paper for the children to draw, scribble, glue, and paint on. Start with drawing paper and lunch bags. Add construction paper, newspaper pages, and sides of old boxes.

Fill the different sections of the BOX with a variety of art supplies. Here are a few ideas to start with. Remember to rotate the supplies often so the children are continually stimulated.

- Crayons, colored markers, or chalk
- Blunt-tipped scissors
- Box of water colors
- Glue/paste
- Paper scraps
- Yarn
- Buttons

- Popsicle sticks
- Sewing scraps
- Cotton balls
- Bottle caps
- Stones

- Foam pieces
- Wood scraps
- Straw bits
- Tiny boxes